George Edward Martin

**Sunday Songs for little Children**

George Edward Martin

**Sunday Songs for little Children**

ISBN/EAN: 9783337181307

Printed in Europe, USA, Canada, Australia, Japan

Cover: Foto ©Thomas Meinert / pixelio.de

More available books at **www.hansebooks.com**

Copyright, 1898, by The Trustees of
The Presbyterian Board of Publication and Sabbath-School Work.

To

### Little Children,

and especially to

### Those Little Ones,

Who have already sung many of these Hymns and Tunes.

## FOREWORD.

THIS book is a growth of love and not a mere manufacture. It is mainly the practical outcome of nearly a score of years of pleasant and watchful work for and with little children. Whatever skill of pen and brush in picture, letter-press and music-score may be evident in the pages of this little volume the children themselves have inspired. The author has plied his pen and brush, carefully written his lines, scored their companion music, and edited the work of helpful friends with a large desire to lead our little ones to sing and to love to sing that which he believes to be of good teaching and fine grain. The best belongs to the Little Children. This book is an honest and loving emphasis of this great fact.

GEORGE EDWARD MARTIN.

# CONTENTS

| | PAGE |
|---|---|
| Jesus, when He was a Child | 6 |
| The Children's Day | 8 |
| "Than old Judea fairer." | |
| The Children's Day | 10 |
| "The children's day broke sweetly o'er." | |
| The Child's Hymn | 12 |
| He is Calling | 14 |
| The Sweet Old Story | 16 |
| A Morning Song | 18 |
| A Morning Hymn of Praise | 20 |
| Jesus is King | 22 |

### The Seasons—

| | |
|---|---|
| Greeting to Spring | 24 |
| The Violet | 26 |
| Springtime | 28 |
| "Tender flowers that early grow." | |
| Springtime | 30 |
| "The happy birds are singing." | |
| Summer | 32 |
| Autumn | 34 |
| Winter | 36 |

### Festivals—

**Advent.**

| | |
|---|---|
| Hear the Shining Angels Sing | 38 |
| "O Little Town of Bethlehem" | 40 |
| When Jesus Came | 42 |
| Child Jesus | 44 |
| Hark, what Mean the Children's Voices | 46 |

**Resurrection.**

| | |
|---|---|
| Easter Morning | 48 |
| Christ is Risen | 50 |
| "Mary to the Saviour's Tomb" | 52 |

**Thanksgiving.**

| | PAGE |
|---|---|
| "Thou Crownest the Year with Thy Goodness" | 54 |
| Giving Thanks | 56 |

### Shepherd Songs—

| | |
|---|---|
| Dear Little Lambs in a Happy Fold | 58 |
| Little Lambs | 60 |
| The Shepherd Leads His Flock | 62 |
| Invitation | 64 |
| Jesus' Little Lamb | 66 |
| Gracious Saviour, Gentle Shepherd | 68 |

### Soldier Songs—

| | |
|---|---|
| I'm a Little Soldier | 70 |
| A Royal Conqueror | 72 |
| The Captain's Call | 74 |

### Missions—

| | |
|---|---|
| The Final Triumph | 76 |
| The Lands that Need the Gospel | 78 |
| See, the Gospel Light is Shining! | 80 |

| | |
|---|---|
| A Cheerful Gift | 82 |
| Happy Town of Salem | 84 |
| The Church Bells | 86 |
| The Lilies and the Cross | 88 |
| The Love of Jesus | 90 |
| The Virgin's Cradle Song | 92 |
| Come, Let our Lives like Jesus' Shine | 94 |
| The Reapers | 96 |
| The Cross and Crown | 98 |
| A Rest Song | 100 |
| Jesus, Meek and Gentle | 102 |
| The Last Song | 104 |

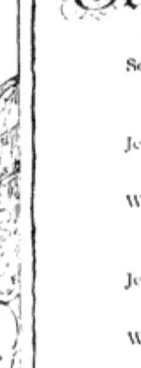

**Jesus**, when He was a child,
  Sought the temple holy;
So do we, His children dear,
  With a spirit lowly.

Jesus, when He was a child,
  Loved the Bible truly;
We would learn, as Jesus did,
  God's dear Word most duly.

Jesus, when He was a child,
  Lived and loved divinely;
We would, like Him, winsome be,
  Live our lives as finely.

Jesus, when He was a child,
  Was the Lord of Glory;
In this house His children dear
  Learn His blessed story.

G. E. M.

## The Children's Day.

THAN old Judea fairer,
   The Church of God to-day!
  Thy little ones still throng to Thee,
O living Lord, alway!
Where Thou dost wait they wander—
  Wayside and city wall,
And field and fen and hilly glen
  Shall answer to Thy call.

Glad seer, that hailed the shining
  Of Zion's light afar!
Our city fair, it hath no need
  Of sun or moon or star.
Its gates are ever open,
  And in and out alway
The boys and girls, with songful lips,
  Keep one long Children's Day.

BURNHAM.

# The Children's Day.

GEORGE A. KIES.

*Moderato.*

1. Than old Judea fairer The Church of God to-day! Thy little ones still throng to Thee, O living Lord alway! Where thou dost wait they wander—Wayside and city wall, And field and fen and hilly glen Shall answer to thy call.

THE Children's Day broke sweetly o'er
　　A weary world repining,
　　When Jesus came to Mary mild,
　　And Christmas stars were shining
　　　　On Children's Day,
　　　　　　The Children's Day,
　　　　　　　　The happy Children's Day!

The Children's Day begins to shine,
　Its morning stars glow faintly;
Its dawn climbs up the sky to noon,
　When earth is growing saintly
　　　For Children's Day,
　　　　The Children's Day,
　　　　　　The happy Children's Day!

O Love divine, we pledge our faith
　To Thee, who loves and feeds us
In heavenly pastures, green and fair,
　Whereto the Christ-Child leads us
　　　On Children's Day,
　　　　The Children's Day,
　　　　　　The happy Children's Day!

The Children's Day is heaven's Great Day,
　In realms of untold glory,
Where angel throngs, in raptured song,
　Repeat the "old, old story"
　　　Of Children's Day,
　　　　The Children's Day,
　　　　　　The happy Children's Day!

　　　　　　　　　　G. E. M.

## A Child's Hymn

"JUST as I am," thine own to be,
    Friend of the young, who lovest me,
    To consecrate myself to Thee,
        O Jesus Christ, I come!

In the glad morning of my days,
My life to give, my vows to pay,
With no reserve and no delay,
    With all my heart, I come.

"Just as I am," young, strong and free,
To be the best that I can be,
For truth and righteousness and Thee,
    Lord of my life, I come.

And for Thy sake to win renown,
And, then, to take my victor's crown,
And at Thy feet to cast it down,
    O Master, Lord, I come!

FARMINGTON.

## The Child's Hymn.

## He is Calling.

CHILDREN, dear, the Saviour's calling,
  While your faith is clear and true;
As of old He sought the children,
Now, His heart goes out to you.

  REFRAIN—He is calling, gently calling,
      Gently calling, child, to you.

He is calling, for He loves you,
  As he called in olden days;
Then the children loved to hear Him,
  And to follow in His ways.
          REFRAIN—

Children, dear, the Saviour's calling,
  Heed His call, as they of old;
Love the Shepherd, He will guide you
  To the restful, heavenly fold.
          REFRAIN—
            G. F. M.

## He is Calling.

G. E. M.

1. Chil-dren dear, the Saviour's call-ing, While your faith is clear and true;
As of old He sought the chil-dren, Now His heart goes out to you.
He is call-ing, gent-ly call-ing, Gent-ly call-ing, child, to you.

## The Sweet Old Story.

I THINK when I read that sweet story of old,
    When Jesus was here among men,
How He called little children like lambs to His fold,
    I should like to have been with Him then.

I wish that His hands had been placed on my head,
    That His arm had been thrown around me,
And that I might have seen His kind look when He said,
    "Let the little ones come unto me."

Yet still to His footstool in prayer I may go,
    And ask for a share in His love;
And if I thus earnestly seek Him below,
    I shall see Him and hear Him above.

## The Sweet Old Story.

GEORGE A. KITS.

1. I think, when I read that sweet story of old, When Jesus was here among men, How He called little children like lambs to His fold, I should like to have been with Him then.

# A Morning Song

SEEK the Saviour early, children dear,
   While the light is shining bright and clear,
   When the shadows dreary draw not near.
Seek Him, for He loves you, do not fear.

  REFRAIN—Seek Him in the dawning,
         Seek Him in the light,
         Children of the morning,
         Children of the light.

Seek to know the Saviour, children dear,
He will lead to fountains ever clear.
For your little feet He knows the way,
As He leads you safely day by day.
                REFRAIN—

Hear the Saviour calling, "O, how true
Is the love I always bear to you!
Follow closely, children, after me,
Till the heavenly pastures you shall see."
                REFRAIN—

# A Morning Song.

G. E. M.

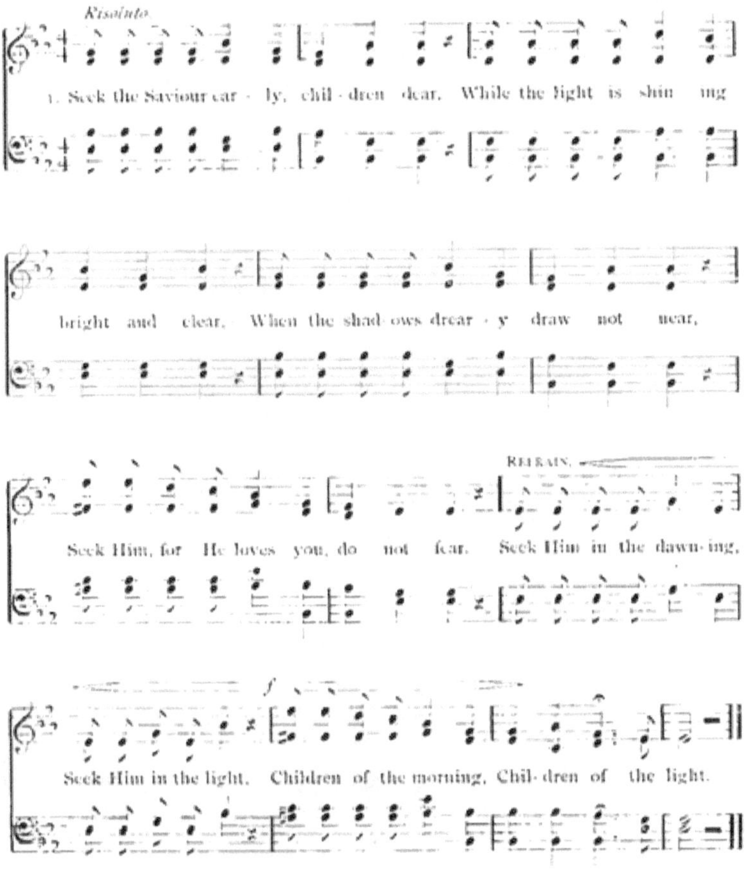

1. Seek the Saviour early, children dear, While the light is shining bright and clear, When the shadows dreary draw not near, Seek Him, for He loves you, do not fear.

REFRAIN.

Seek Him in the dawning, Seek Him in the light, Children of the morning, Children of the light.

## A Morning Hymn of Praise.

THE sun is on the land and sea,
   The day begun;
Our morning hymn begins with Thee,
   Blest three in one;
Our praise shall rise continuously
   Till day is done.

Thy love was ever in our view,
   Like stars by night;
Thy gifts are every morning new,
   O God of Light;
Thy mercy, like the heavens blue,
   Fills all our sight.

We do not know what grief or care
   The day may bring;
The heart shall find some gladness there
   That loves its king;
The life that serves Thee everywhere
   Can always sing.

                              BENSON.

## Jesus is King.

COME, little children, your praises sing.
    Jesus is king! Jesus is king!
Give Him your hearts as an offering,
    Jesus is king! Jesus is king!
Now in the morning, when life is bright,
Walk with the Saviour, His children of light;
Come, little children, your praises sing,
    Jesus is king! Jesus is king!

Come, little children, your voices raise,
    Sing forth His praise, sing forth His praise;
Children of olden days sang their lays,
    Sing forth His praise, sing forth His praise.
Sing, like the children of days gone by,
Sing, for a singing Messiah draws nigh;
Come, little children, your voices raise,
    Sing forth His praise, sing forth His praise.

Happy the children, wherein they sing,
    Jesus is king! Jesus is king!
Safe in His care and His shepherding,
    Jesus is king! Jesus is king!
Lambs love the shepherds and His dear fold,
His love for the children can never be told,
Happy the children whene'er they sing
    Jesus is king! Jesus is king!

                              G. F. M.

## Greeting to Spring.

LIGHTLY in my heart they sing,
   Joy bells softly pealing;
Ring out, little songs of spring,
   Through the wide world stealing.

To the budding violets fly,
   Make their fragrance sweeter;
And, if thou a rose espy,
   Say I bid thee greet her.

GERMAN.

## The Violet.

AH, violet, dearest violet,
    Will you not tell me, dear,
Why you are here so early,
    Ere other flowers appear?

"Because I am so tiny,
    Therefore in May come I;
If I came with the others,
    I fear you'd pass me by."

The smallest flower that blossoms
    Our Father knoweth well;
How much he loves its beauty,
    Ah, who can truly tell!

GERMAN.

## Springtime.

TENDER flowers, that early grow,
Their Creator's praises show;
In their fragrant, winsome way,
This is what they seem to say—
"Children, dear, you are God's spring,
Sweeten, brighten every thing."

Modest flowers, that early bloom,
Seem to fade away so soon;
Yet, in brave and hopeful way,
This is what they seem to say—
"Children, dear, lose not your spring,
Sweeten, brighten every thing."

Immortelles God's children are,
Bright with beauty from afar;
From His glorious heavenly ways,
This is what the Saviour says—
"Children, dear, your hearts give me,
Bloom for immortality."

G. E. M.

## Springtime.

### Springtime.

happy birds are singing,
Oh, let the children listen
 To their song ;
"From sunny climes we're winging,
From days that glow and glisten,
 All day long."

REFRAIN—Oh, children, lift your hearts to sing
To Him who brings the wondrous spring.
The springtime, the springtime,
The happy, happy springtime,
The springtime, the springtime,
The happy, happy spring.

The children, too, are singing,
The happy hours are filling
 With their song ;
"We come to Jesus bringing
A service, glad and willing,
 All day long."—REFRAIN.

G. E. M.

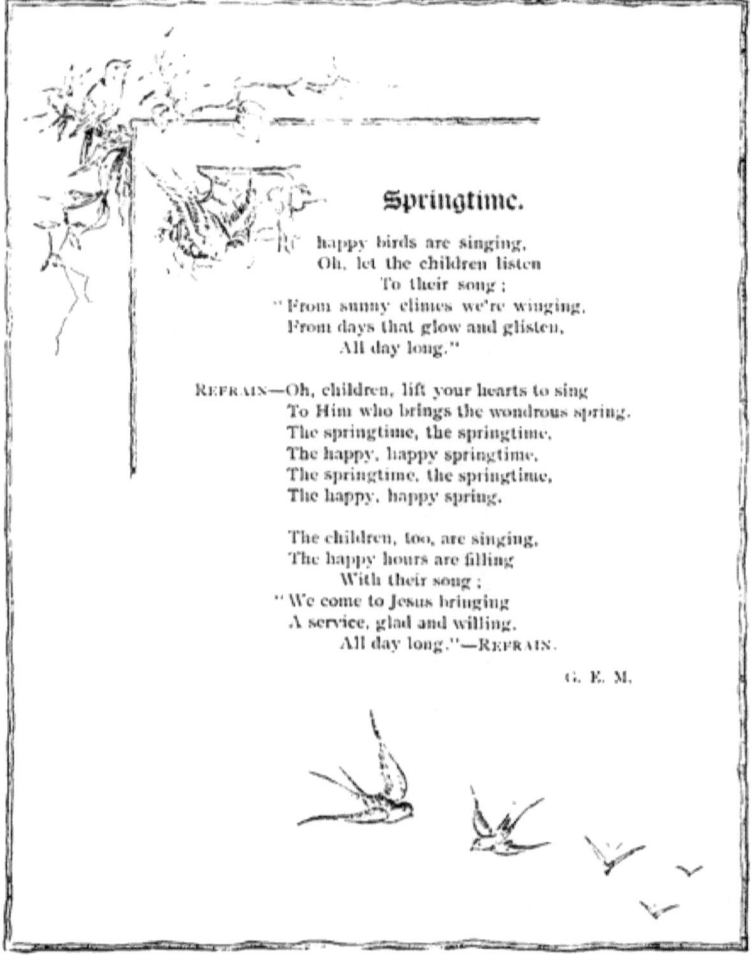

## Summer.

WHEN summer floods the earth with light,
The day is long and short the night;
The children love to sing and play
Throughout the livelong sunny day.

The children are life's summer day,
Whose hours are filled with happy play,
With Faith and Hope and heavenly Love,
God sends to cheer us from above.

The children often sought His smile,
Who loved and blessed them all the while
He trod this earth with human feet,
And made the ways of toil more sweet.

The children love His kindly face
That shines for them in every place,
And makes a constant summer where
Were else, sad darkness and despair.

G. E. M.

## Summer.

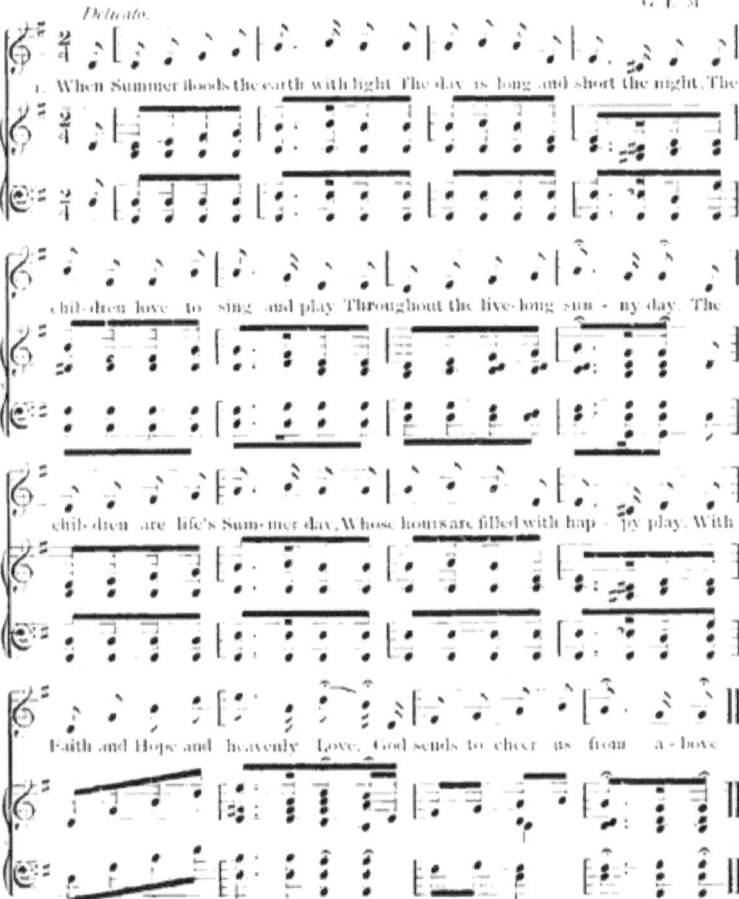

## Autumn.

THE mellow sun is shining
  Over golden fields;
To harvest song and reaper
  The ripened harvest yields;
The Summer birds are thinking
  Of climes that mellow are;
The long sun ever shineth
  In Southland, fair and far.

The laden trees are bending,
  With luscious fruit bowed down;
Of all the royal colors,
  Kind Nature wears her crown.
The children should be thinking,
  In this, their summer hour,
Of harvest after sunshine,
  Of fruit to follow flower.

Sweet Autumn days are holding—
  The year is growing old—
The glory of the summer,
  In fields of waving gold.
O children, who love Jesus,
  Your life and light and crown,
Keep clear and bright His sunshine,
  Through all the long years down.

G. E. M.

## Autumn.

G. E. M.

35

## Winter.

When the wind blows cold,
   And the year grows old,
The soft white snow's descending;
  Weary Nature sleeps,
  While "Our Father" keeps
His watch o'er all, defending.

When the wind blows cold,
And the year grows old,
The fires of home are gleaming;
  Winter's icy face
  Finds no welcome place
In light from firesides streaming.

When the wind blows cold,
And the year grows old,
The children must keep shining:
  They are life's bright glow,
  In whose light we know
Where clouds hide silver lining.    G. E. M.

## A Christmas Song

Dear the shining angels sing,
"Peace on earth, goodwill we bring,
Let the light of Christmas morn
Flood the saddened hearts that mourn."

REFRAIN—Christ the Lord is born to-day,
Oh, happy Christmas Day!

Glorious was the heavenly light,
Streaming through the wintry night;
Glorious was the Babe Divine,
Laid in lowly manger shrine.

REFRAIN—

Weary world, your conflicts cease,
Listen to the song of peace,
Learn to sing the angel song—
Peace for war and truth for wrong.

REFRAIN—

As the length'ning years glide on,
May we heed this heavenly song,
'Till at last, in perfect rest,
We shall sing among the blest.

REFRAIN—

## "O Little Town of Bethlehem."

O LITTLE town of Bethlehem!
  How still we see thee lie,
Above thy deep and dreamless sleep,
  The silent stars go by;
Yet in thy dark streets shineth
  The Everlasting Light;
The hopes and fears of all the years
  Are met in thee to-night.

For Christ is born of Mary,
  And gathered all above,
While mortals sleep, the angels keep
  Their watch of wondering love.
O morning stars together
  Proclaim the holy birth!
And praises sing to God the king,
  And peace to men on earth.

How silently, how silently,
  The wondrous gift is given;
So God imparts to human hearts
  The blessings of His heaven;
No ear may hear His coming,
  But in this world of sin,
Where meek souls will receive Him still,
  The dear Christ enters in.

O holy child of Bethlehem!
  Descend to us, we pray,
Cast out our sin and enter in,
  Be born in us to-day.
We hear the Christmas angels
  The great glad tidings tell;
O, come to us, abide with us,
  Our Lord Immanuel!

PHILIPS BROOKS.

## When Jesus Came.

LONG years ago, by Bethlehem town,
   The temple sheep were feeding,
The wintry stars shone kindly down
   On flock and shepherds heeding,
     When Jesus came.

The wise men from the orient,
   Led by a starry finger,
The shepherds, too, by angels sent
   To worship did not linger,
     When Jesus came.

A mother's love received its crown
   And childhood dearest blessing,
When Heaven's King did nestle down
   In Mary's arms, caressing,
     When Jesus came.

O happy night, so full of song
   And joy for every sorrow!
For stars shine bright, though nights be long,
   And dawns a glad to-morrow,
     Since Jesus came.

                G. E. M.

## "Child Jesus."

CHILD Jesus came from heavenly height,
   To make us pure and holy,
On bed of straw on Christmas night,
   He lay in manger lowly;
The star smiled down from heaven to greet,
The oxen kissed the baby feet.
   Hallelujah! Hallelujah! Child Jesus!

All sorrow and all care lay down,
   And praise the Lord of heaven;
"A child is born in David's town,
   To us a son is given:"
Like children, let us kneel before
The Holy Christ-Child and adore.
   Hallelujah! Hallelujah! Child Jesus!

GORMAN.

# Child Jesus.

GERMAN.  
Moderato.  
GEORGE A. KIES.

Child Jesus came from heavenly height, To make us pure and holy, On bed of straw on Christmas night, He lay in manger lowly: The star smiled down from heaven to greet, The oxen kissed the baby feet. Hallelujah! Hallelujah! Hallelujah! Child Jesus!

## Hark! What Mean the Children's Voices?

H ARK! what mean the children's voices,
   Sweetly sounding forth in praise?
Lo, a happy band rejoices,
   Hear them chant their blessed lays.

Hear them tell the wondrous story,
   Hear the happy children cry
That a child was Lord of Glory,
   Glory be to God on high!

Christ has come, the Great Anointed,
   Let the children praises sing;
Let them love whom God appointed
   For their Prophet, Priest and King.

    "See, His star is shining o'er us!"
      Lo, the blessed children cry;
    Soon, in heaven, He'll shine before us.
      Glory be to God on high!

                    G. E. M.

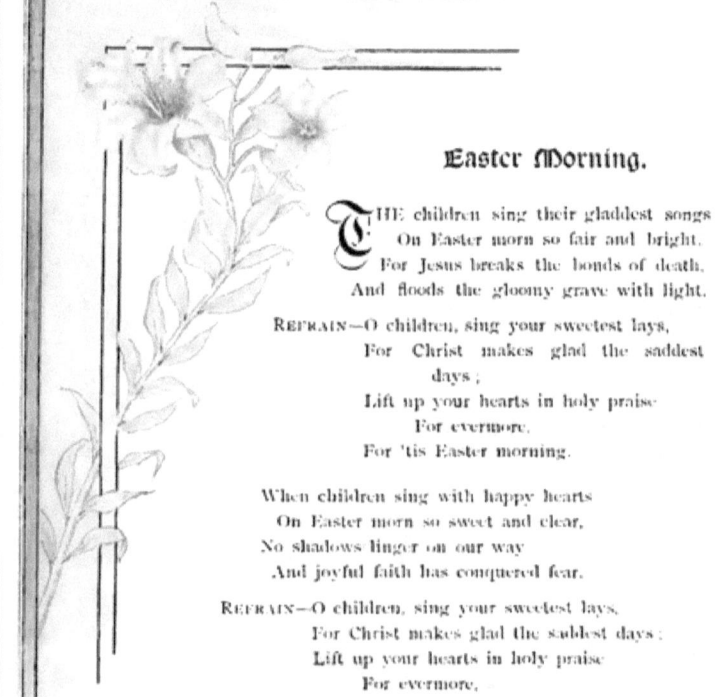

## Easter Morning.

THE children sing their gladdest songs
   On Easter morn so fair and bright,
For Jesus breaks the bonds of death,
And floods the gloomy grave with light.

REFRAIN—O children, sing your sweetest lays,
   For Christ makes glad the saddest days;
   Lift up your hearts in holy praise
     For evermore,
   For 'tis Easter morning.

When children sing with happy hearts
On Easter morn so sweet and clear,
No shadows linger on our way
And joyful faith has conquered fear.

REFRAIN—O children, sing your sweetest lays,
   For Christ makes glad the saddest days;
   Lift up your hearts in holy praise
     For evermore,
   For 'tis Easter morning.

                          G. E. M.

## Christ is Risen.

HEAR the happy children as they sing,
    Hear them sing, hear them sing;
Hear the blessed news the angels bring—
Christ is risen, Christ is King.
The heavy stone is rolled away,
The grave's dark night gives place to day,
For Christ is risen indeed.

REFRAIN—Hear the happy bells of Easter morn—
    Christ is risen, Christ is risen;
Hear the blessed message, sweet and strong—
    Christ is risen, Christ is risen.

Hear the happy children as they sing,
    Hear them sing, hear them sing;
Hear the blessed news the angels bring—
Christ is risen, Christ is King.
For death has lost His awful sway,
Bright angels guard the tomb alway,
For Christ is risen indeed.

REFRAIN—Hear the happy bells of Easter morn—
    Christ is risen, Christ is risen;
Hear the blessed message, sweet and strong—
    Christ is risen, Christ is risen.

                    G. E. M.

## Mary to the Saviour's Tomb.

MARY to the Saviour's tomb
   Hastened at the early dawn;
Spice she brought and sweet perfume,
   But the Lord she loved had gone.
There awhile she weeping stood,
   Asking where her Saviour lay;
Tears she wept, a bitter flood,
   Lost in anguish and dismay.

Soon her sorrow all was gone,
   When she heard His own dear voice

Call her "Mary!" Oh, that
   tone!
How it bade her heart re-
   joice!
Such a change His Word can
   make,
Turning darkness into day;
Ye who weep for Jesus'
   sake,
He will wipe your tears
   away.

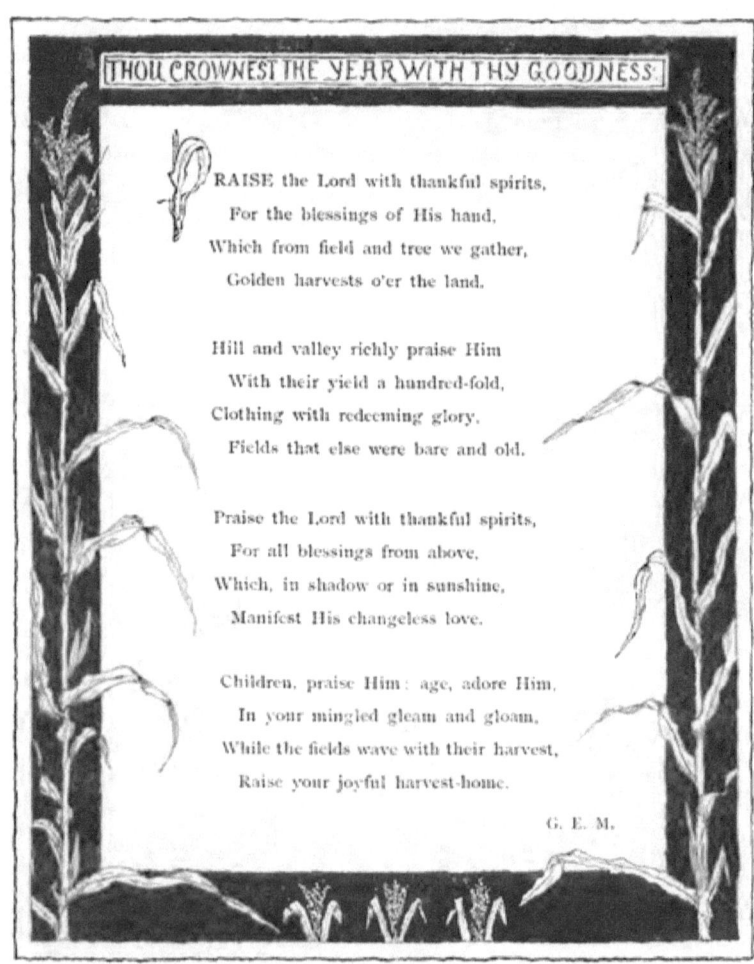

**THOU CROWNEST THE YEAR WITH THY GOODNESS**

PRAISE the Lord with thankful spirits,
    For the blessings of His hand,
Which from field and tree we gather,
    Golden harvests o'er the land.

Hill and valley richly praise Him
    With their yield a hundred-fold,
Clothing with redeeming glory,
    Fields that else were bare and old.

Praise the Lord with thankful spirits,
    For all blessings from above,
Which, in shadow or in sunshine,
    Manifest His changeless love.

Children, praise Him; age, adore Him,
    In your mingled gleam and gloam,
While the fields wave with their harvest,
    Raise your joyful harvest-home.

                        G. E. M.

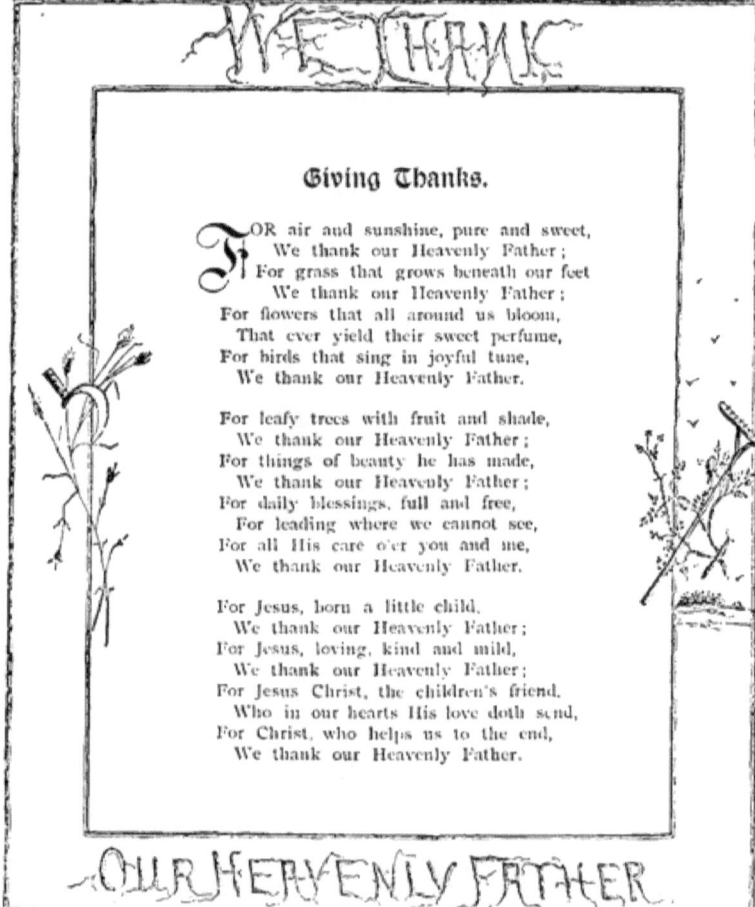

### Giving Thanks.

FOR air and sunshine, pure and sweet,
   We thank our Heavenly Father;
For grass that grows beneath our feet
   We thank our Heavenly Father;
For flowers that all around us bloom,
   That ever yield their sweet perfume,
For birds that sing in joyful tune,
   We thank our Heavenly Father.

For leafy trees with fruit and shade,
   We thank our Heavenly Father;
For things of beauty he has made,
   We thank our Heavenly Father;
For daily blessings, full and free,
   For leading where we cannot see,
For all His care o'er you and me,
   We thank our Heavenly Father.

For Jesus, born a little child,
   We thank our Heavenly Father;
For Jesus, loving, kind and mild,
   We thank our Heavenly Father;
For Jesus Christ, the children's friend,
   Who in our hearts His love doth send,
For Christ, who helps us to the end,
   We thank our Heavenly Father.

## Dear Little Lambs in a Happy Fold.

DEAR little lambs in a happy fold!
Jesus will keep them from harm and cold,
Following, truly, quite close to Him,
Wandering not in the ways of sin.

Come, little children, sing out your praise,
Sing unto Jesus your sweetest lays;
Lambs will He gather with loving arm,
Shelter them ever from sin and harm.

Come, little children, heed the call
Jesus is making for one and all;
Haste, in the morning of life, to be
Close to the Shepherd, who loveth thee.

"Jesus, we come to Thy loving care,
Lead us in pastures both rich and fair,
Shepherd the children while here
    below,
Loving and trusting the Shepherd so."

G. E. M.

## Little Lambs.

LITTLE lambs, so white and fair,
Are the Shepherd's constant care;
Now He leads their tender feet
Into pastures green and sweet.

How they listen and obey,
Following where He leads the way;
Heavenly Father, may we be
Thus obedient unto Thee.

## The Shepherd Leads His Flock.

THE Shepherd leads His flock
   Where the pleasant waters glide;
His sheep are always safe
   When they follow by His side.

In every faithful life
   Are pastures fair and green,
Where Jesus folds His sheep
   By silver waters' gleam.

Oh, wondrous fair the heart
   Where Jesus' love abounds!
A fragrant, fruitful land
   Of beauteous lights and sounds.

A child may early know
   This peace of Jesus' love,
A surety of rest
   In pastures fair above.

           G. E. M.

## Invitation.

"SUFFER the children," the Saviour said,
    When in Jewry He taught so truly;
Still He is calling the children dear,
    Let us heed His sweet call most duly.
He calls in the morning, when life is pure,
    His love for the children is winning,
He calls to His lambs with His sweetest voice,
    He calls when the day is beginning.

Surely the children will heed His care,
    For He loveth His lambs most dearly;
Out from the ways and the woes of sin,
    How gently He calls and clearly!
"Dear lambs, seek my side while the morning lasts,
    Dear lambs, find the fold ere the gloaming;
See, here is the staff! See, here is the love
    That keepeth the children from roaming!"

G. F. M.

## Jesus' Little Lamb.

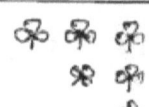

JESUS' little lamb am I,
On His goodness I rely,
He, my gentle Shepherd, leads me
In His pastures green He feeds me,
For He loves me, knows me well,
And my little name can tell.

Underneath His gracious staff
I go in and out, and have
Pastures sweet around me lying,
Still my hungry soul supplying;
When I thirst, my feet He brings
Where the living water springs.

Should a lambkin, then, like me,
Ever sad and thankless be?
When these pleasant days are ended,
On my Shepherd's bosom tended,
I shall go to perfect bliss;
O, no joy can equal this!

G. E. M.

GRACIOUS Saviour, gentle Shepherd,
    Little ones are dear to Thee;
Gathered with Thine arms and carried
    In Thy bosom may we be,
Sweetly, fondly, safely tended,
    From all want and danger free.

Cleanse our hearts from sinful folly
    In the stream Thy love supplied,
Mingled stream of blood and water,
    Flowing from Thy wounded side;

And to heavenly pastures lead us,
    Where Thine own still waters glide.

Taught to lisp Thy holy praises
    Which on earth Thy children sing,
Both with lips and hearts unfeigned,
    May we our thank-offerings bring;
Then, with all the saints in glory,
    Join to praise our Lord and King.

BICKERSTETH.

## Gracious Saviour, Gentle Shepherd.

## A Little Soldier.

I'M a little soldier of the Cross,
   And I love my Captain, good and strong,
When He leads to battle I will go
   Onward into victory with this song—
REFRAIN—I'm a little soldier of the Cross,
         Jesus is my Captain, I've no fear;
         How can cruel Satan do me harm
         When my loving Saviour's ever near?

I'm a little soldier of the Cross,
   "Little children, lead them," saith the King;
Onward into battle let us go,
   Onward into victory as we sing—
           REFRAIN—

I'm a little soldier of the Cross,
   Faithful to my Captain I will be;
When the time of heavenly peace shall come,
   Then my Captain's loving face I'll see.
           REFRAIN—

                      G. E. M.

## A Royal Conqueror.

THE Son of God goes forth to war,
   A kingly crown to gain;
His blood-red banner streams afar,
   Who follows in His train?
Who best can drink his cup of woe,
   Triumphant over pain,
Who patient bears his cross below,
   He follows in His train.

A noble army, men and boys,
   The matron and the maid,
Around the Saviour's throne rejoice,
   In robes of light arrayed:
They climbed the steep ascent of heaven
   Through peril, toil and pain;
O God, to us may grace be given
   To follow in their train.

REGINALD HEBER.

## A Royal Conqueror.

G. E. M.

1. The Son of God goes forth to war, A kingly crown to gain; His blood-red banner streams afar, Who follows in His train? Who best can drink his cup of woe, Triumphant over pain, Who patient bears his Cross below, He follows in His train.

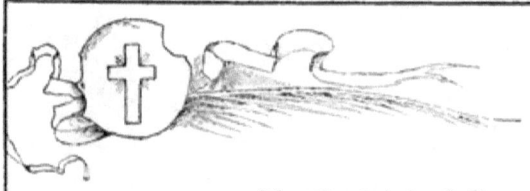

## The Captain's Call.

H EAR the Captain clearly calling,
   While our lives are young and strong,
"Fall in line, my youthful soldiers;
   Up, for the battle, with this song—
REFRAIN—We are soldiers of the Cross,
         With our Captain we will fight;
         Down forever, prince of sin!
         Up forever, Prince of Light!"

Hear our Captain clearly calling,
   To us all his summons ring,
"Faint not, comrades, in the battle;
   As ye struggle, shout and sing—
        REFRAIN—

We shall hear the Captain calling
   Softly, when the fight is won,
"Fall in line, my faithful soldiers,
   You have won the great 'Well done.'"
        REFRAIN—

                G. E. M.

## The Final Triumph.

HARK! what mean those wondrous voices!
  Heaven's high arches ring with song:
As a mighty host rejoices,
  Crowned saints their praise prolong:
See them wave their palms in glory,
  Hear them sing of Jesus' strife,
Hear them chant the sad, great story,
  How in death He brought us life.

Children, sing with happy voices,
  As celestial triumphs ring:
Let the psalm, that heaven rejoices,
  In your loyal hearts begin.
God shall brighten every station
  Where the Cross of Christ shall be
Light and shelter for the nation,
  By his wondrous love made free.

                        G. E. M.

## The Lands that need the Gospel.

FOR lands that need the gospel
   The children toil and pray,
That they who know Christ's story
   May tell it there alway.

For lands that shone with glory
   When Christmas music rung;
For lands where, ages after,
   This song of life begun.

For northlands drear and ice-bound,
   For southlands of the palm,
For all earth's weary places
   They lift their prayer and psalm.

They pray that Jesus' coming
   May fill the earth with light,
That peace shall conquer discord,
   And wrong give place to right.

G. E. M.

## The Lands that need the Gospel.

G. E. M.

## See, the Gospel Light is Shining!

SEE, the gospel light is shining
  Far beyond that verdant hill,
Where the Son, his own resigning,
  Kept the Father's holy will.
Many are the lands that know Him,
  Many are the eyes that see,
Many are the hearts that show Him
  Glad and constant loyalty.

    Swift, the day is surely spreading
      When, in every waiting clime,
    Day shall break, sin's night receding,
      Everywhere the Christ shall shine:
    Every land shall know His glory,
      Every soul shall see His face;
    Haste to spread the wondrous story
      Of His world-redeeming grace.

G. E. M.

## A Cheerful Gift.

A CHEERFUL gift, a cheerful gift,
   Come, children, bring to Jesus!
   How much He gave for each of you—
   His life, so great and kind and true!
   And, now, what will the children do
      To show their love for Jesus?

A cheerful gift, a cheerful gift,
They'll bring whom Jesus calleth.
From hearts of love and willing hands,
From all the little children bands,
In this and many other lands,
    What blessed gifts are falling!

                      G. E. M.

## A Cheerful Gift.

GEORGE A. KIES.

1. A cheer-ful gift, a cheer-ful gift, Come, children, bring to Je-sus! How much He gave for each of you— His life, so great and kind and true! And, now, what will the chil-dren do To show their love to Je-sus?

HAPPY town of Salem!
   Happy little feet
Of the children playing
   In the golden street!
"Let them come," says Jesus,
   "And forbid them not:"
But the proud in Salem
   Have no part nor lot.

Happy town of Salem
   With its open gates!
Happy are the pilgrims
   Whom a welcome waits!
In the name of Jesus
   They an entrance claim,
And the guards of Salem
   Answer, "In His name."

Happy town of Salem,
   Vision true of peace,
Seen above earth's strivings,
   Steadfast when they cease!
"Take thy cross," says Jesus;
   And the narrow way
Brings the feet to Salem
   At the break of day.

                     BENSON.

## The Church Bells.

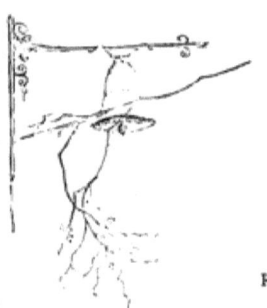

THE church bells! the church bells!
How much their blessed music tells
Of holy day God gives to men,
To learn His truth and, ever, then
To listen to His gracious word
And love and live as they have heard.

REFRAIN—The church bells! the church bells!
How much their blessed music tells!

The church bells! the church bells!
How much their gentle music tells
Of that which waits for children dear,
Of joy and love that know no fear,
If they obey the Saviour's call,
And heed His message over all.

REFRAIN—The church bells! the church bells!
How much their gentle music tells!

The church bells! the church bells!
How much their joyful music tells!
It ringeth in a fuller song,
That we shall all enjoy ere long:
Soon, earthly bells must cease to ring
And heaven's glad music will begin.

REFRAIN—The church bells! the church bells!
How much their joyful music tells!

G. E. M.

# The Church Bells.

## The Lilies and the Cross.

THE lilies are not whiter
   Than the heart of Him who died
   That sinful souls might cleansed be
In Calvary's crimson tide;

That, as the Christ hath suffered,
   They, too, must suffer loss,
The sign of their sweet purity—
   White lilies by a cross.

How rich and rare the reaches
   The heavenly gardener knows,
Where bloom of white, with heart of gold,
   His gracious life-blood shows!

Dear Christ, teach us the secret
   Of grace by keenest loss,
That we may grow to be as white
   As lilies by a cross.

            G. E. M.

## The Lilies and the Cross.

GEORGE A. KIES.

1. The lil - ies are not whit - er Than the heart of Him who died, That sin - ful souls might cleans - ed be In Cal - vary's crim - son tide; That as the Christ hath suf - fered, They, too, must suf - fer loss, The sign of their sweet pu - ri - ty—White lil - ies by a cross.

## THE LOVE OF JESUS

SWEETLY sing the love of Jesus,
  Love for you and love for me;
Heaven's light is not more cheering,
  Heaven's dews are not more free.
As a child, in pain or terror,
  Hides him in his mother's breast,
As a sailor seeks his haven,
  We would come to Him for rest.

Gladly sing the love of Jesus,
  Let us lean upon His arm :
If He loves us what can grieve us?
  If He keeps us what can harm?
Still He lays His hands in blessing
  On each timid little face,
And in heaven the children's angels
  Near the throne have always place.

Ever sing the love of Jesus,
  Let the day be dark or clear,
Every pain and every sorrow
  Bring His own to Him more near.
Death's cold wave need not affright us
  When we know that He has died,
When we see the face of Jesus
  Smiling on the other side.

MARY VIRGINIA TERHUNE.

## The Virgin's Cradle Song.

THE Virgin stills the crying
Of Jesus, sleepless lying,
And singing for his pleasure,
Thus calls upon her treasure,
"My darling, do not weep,
My Jesus, sleep!"

"My child of might indwelling,
My sweet all sweets excelling,
Of bliss the fountain flowing,
The Day Spring ever flowing,
My darling, do not weep,
My Jesus, sleep!"

"Say, would'st thou heavenly sweetness,
Or love of answering meetness,
Or is fit music wanting?
Ho! angels, raise your chanting!
My darling, do not weep,
My Jesus, sleep!"

FROM A LATIN HYMN.

### Come, let our Lives like Jesus' Shine.

LONG years ago, in David's town,
　　The darkness gently falling,
　　Was heard by wondering temple throngs
　　　The voice of Jesus calling—
"I am the dark world's blessed light;"
　　No other is so healing,
Hark! how it sounds through all the years,
　　So clear and so appealing!

It speaks to all who love the light
　　And do not fear its shining,
Which searches every human heart,
　　The good in each divining.
Come, let our lives like Jesus' shine,
　　In pleasure or in sadness,
To glow through all our coming days
　　With patience and with gladness.

　　　　　　　　　　G. E. M.

## The Reapers.

THE fields are white to harvest,
    They wave with precious grain;
The reapers' song and sickle
    We hear and see again.
The children may not gather
    As busy reapers, strong,
But they can cheer the toilers
    With happy harvest song.

"Put in the sickle, reapers,
    The sickle keen and bright.
On level plain and hillside
    Ere falls the silent night:"
To all God's earnest toilers
    The children friends have been;
Their harvest-home shall sweeten
    The rest His workmen win.

                      G. E. M.

## The Cross and Crown.

THE Cross and Crown! the Cross and Crown!
The patient Saviour bore them
'Mid keen reproach and bitter scorn,
The heavy Cross and Crown of thorn;
O, patient souls in darkest storm,
For His dear sake adore them!

The Cross and Crown! the Cross and Crown!
Thy glory none can sunder;
The Cross has changed to great white throne,
For hurt of thorns a crown atones,
And happy souls, on lifted thrones,
    Sing of the heavenly wonder.

The Cross and Crown! the Cross and Crown!
In faithful lives they're shining;
When days are bright, when days are dark,
When hope is dumb or like the lark;
The faithful in the stillness hark,
    A song of heaven divining.

                                                G. E. M.

## A Rest Song.

WHEN night is gently falling,
   And stars begin to shine,
A weary world is resting
   Safe in a love divine.
And, so, when shadows deepen,
   And nature sinks to rest,
I trust the care of Jesus,
   Who little children blessed.

E'er since the stars were shining
   On Bethlehem's cradle throne,
O'er all the sleeping children
   The love of God hath shone.
And, so, when shadows deepen
   And stars shine clear and bright,
I rest while Jesus watches
   Throughout the quiet night.

G. E. M.

# JESUS, meek and gentle.

JESUS, meek and gentle,
  Son of God most high,
Pitying, loving Saviour,
  Hear Thy children's cry.

Give us holy freedom,
  Fill our hearts with love;
Draw us, holy Jesus,
  To the realms above.

Lead us on our journey,
  Be Thyself the way,
Through this earthly darkness
  To celestial day.

PRYNNE.

## The Last Song.

JESUS, tender Shepherd, hear me,
  Bless Thy little child to-night;
Through the darkness be Thou near
    me,
  Watch my sleep till morning light.

All this day Thy hand hath led me,
  And I thank Thee for Thy care;
Thou hast clothed me, warmed and fed me,
  Listen to my evening prayer.

Let my sins be all forgiven,
  Bless the friends I love so well;
Take me, when I die, to heaven,
  Happy there with Thee to dwell.

www.ingramcontent.com/pod-product-compliance
Lightning Source LLC
Chambersburg PA
CBHW030409170426
43202CB00010B/1542